HURON COUNTY PUBLIC LIBRARY

W9-CIB-587

# THE BIRCH BARK CAPER

# STANLEY BURKE * ROY PETERSON

Douglas & McIntyre
Vancouver / Toronto

NOV 30 '81

71677

Text copyright © 1981 by Stanley Burke
Drawings copyright © 1981 by Roy Peterson

All rights reserved. No part of this book may be
reproduced or transmitted in any form by any
means without permission in writing from the
publisher, except by a reviewer, who may quote
brief passages in a review.

Douglas & McIntyre Ltd.
1615 Venables Street
Vancouver, British Columbia

Canadian Cataloguing in Publication Data

Burke, Stanley, 1923-
    The birchbark caper

    ISBN 0-88894-306-7

    1. Canada - Politics and government -
1980-        - Anecdotes, facetiae, satire, etc.*
I. Peterson, Roy, 1936-        II. Title.
FC173.B87        971.064'6'0207        C81-091292-9
F1026.4.B87

Cover art by Roy Peterson
Printed and bound in Canada by John Deyell Company

The Swamp had a new and terrible problem—all the other animals were getting richer than the Beavers.

"It's not fair," said the Beavers. "It's downright un-Swampian."

The Beavers, you see, had always been richer than anybody else. They had conquered the Frogs long ago; then they had built the wonderful Dam that made the Swamp secure. Finally, they had invented the Gliberal Party. The lesser animals in the far reaches of the Swamp had benefited from these works and, gratefully, they had rewarded the Beavers.

"We look after the Swamp and the Swamp looks after us," said the Beavers cheerfully.

"*Noblesse oblige,*\*" said the Gliberals.

This was the way of the Swamp. And so, thought the Beavers, it would always be.

But suddenly, it wasn't.

Everything had changed and it was all the fault of Swampoil.

\* An old Frog saying which loosely translated means "Oblige the Gliberals."

It started with the wily Camels in faraway Ah-Rob-Ya when Sheik Yer-Money put prices up. The Marmots whistled and put theirs up, too. The Marmots lived near the Great Western Hills on the far side of the Swamp and owned vast amounts of this expensive stuff which came out of the ground and which everyone needed. Indeed, the Beavers needed it to stay rich and were outraged at the disloyalty of the Marmots.

The Marmots, however, explained that all the Swamp would benefit if they became richer—and the Ordinary Animals sighed and said they'd heard that before somewhere.

Meanwhile, the Marmots' neighbours in the Great Meadowland, the Gophers, were also becoming rich because they, too, had Swampoil. They also had some funny stuff called You-Rain-On-'Em which everyone in the world wanted—as long as they didn't have to live near it.

The Otters, who lived beyond the Great Western Hills, were becoming even richer than their fish and their forests had made them, because of a black rock that they dug out of the ground, and a dam which was bigger than that of the Beavers. They were also selling land to wealthy foreign animals, making Otters like Nelson Scalpmania richer than the richest Beavers. This allowed Scalpmania and his friends, in turn, to begin buying up much of the eastern part of the Swamp.

Worse than that, these western animals *enjoyed* having money. And the richer they got, the more they laughed at the staid Beavers who thought money was serious and should be put in Banks. And the more they disliked the Gliberals.

"Did you hear," the Beavers said, "that there are only two Gliberals left in all the west? They've been put in a zoo as an endangered species."

To the east, meanwhile, the Codfish were finding Swampoil at a place called High-Burnia. It seemed, after years of being the poorest animals in the Swamp, that they were going to be even richer than the Marmots.

And far to the north in the Blowforth Sea, dynamic animals were rushing around finding more Swampoil, and among the most energetic were two Marmots, Jack Galloper of the Gnome Swampoil Company and Bob Flair of Dusky Swampoil. Great wooden pipelines were being built, and everywhere the Marmots' Swampoil machines were churning furiously. They also had a huge project called Sin-Crude, run by Imperious Oil, which cost a billion

clams and would made them richer still.

Animals the world over hastened to the Land of the Marmots to become rich, too. Even the Bank of Mound Royal (the First Swampian Bank) left the land of the Frogs to set up its headquarters at Call-Girlie where they built the tallest lodge in the western part of the Swamp.

All of this made the Beavers miserable, but the cruellest blow was that even the Frogs were getting richer. The Frogs, having been conquered, were expected to be poor. But the Gliberals had poured so many clams into the shallow end of the Swamp that the Frogs were starting to get rich. This was supposed to make them grateful but, unreliable as ever, the Frogs took the clams and ignored the Beavers.

It seemed nobody needed the Beavers any more, except the Gliberals.

"We are the *nouveau poor!*" cried the Beavers and, in desperation, they turned to their old friends, the Banks.

The Beavers had practically invented Banks and over the years had faithfully brought their offerings to these great Temples of Finance. More than any other animals in the world, the Beavers worshipped and protected their Banks, making sure no evil befell them. The Banks accordingly prospered and their lodges grew higher and higher, each Bank outdoing the other in the magnificence of its temple.

"Now, in our time of need, the Great Banks will not forsake us," said the Beavers. "Remember all their friendly commercials."

Alas, the Banks, having taken everybody's clams for so many years, now refused to give them back.

"It's the Interest Rapes," they explained. "It's too complicated for you to understand; you'll just have to get used to being poor—after all, *someone* has to be poor."

What made the Beavers unhappier still was having to watch as wealthy workers all over the Swamp went on special long vacations called Strikes. Strikes were an invention perfected in the Land of the Otters during which the animals went for long walks and, in the evenings, sat around campfires singing rousing songs. One of their favourites was the grand old labour song, "We Shall Not Be Moved."

The workers were taught how to strike by footloose organizations known as Bunions, so called because of the pain they caused all the other animals. The largest and most progressive Bunion was that of the Bureaucrabs and Snivel Serpents— the United Swampian Loyal Employees Association, commonly known as USLES. Everywhere in the Swamp, USLES officials worked tirelessly to ensure that no government worker became strained or overtaxed.

"Many hands make slight work," the USLES officials liked to say.

Among the best strikers were the Postal Animals, who regularly went on vacation in the summer and at Christmas. This had the benefit, they said, of bringing business to a halt during holiday periods. It also prevented the animals from receiving bad news.

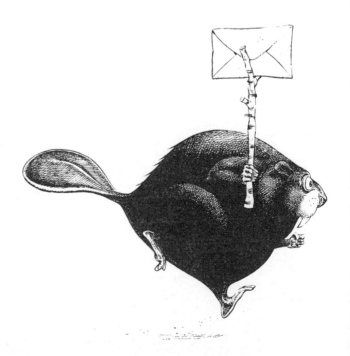

During these vacations, the Postal Animals played a wonderful game called Roulette, after André Roulette, the Chief Postal Animal. In this game, they would dance round and round in circles with animals called Mediators until, finally, the Mediators became tired and fell down. The most extraordinary thing about the game was that no one ever lost—except the non-Postal Animals who, of course, were never asked to play.

The All-Swamp Broadcasting

Corporation went on strike, too, but—somewhat disappointingly—no one noticed.

Everyone was having fun and making clams—except the Ordinary Beavers. Worse still, the Beavers found they had become so poor that the other animals were beginning to feel sorry for them. There was even talk of sending Christmas hampers to needy Beavers.

This was too much. Something had to be done.

So Peter Waterhole promised he would act.

The matter was vital for the Gliberals because their system required the support of the Beavers and, to a lesser extent, the Frogs.

"Look after the Beavers and Frogs and the rest of the Swamp will look after itself," William Lyin' Mackenzie Sting had told them long ago.

"I will save the Beavers!" Peter Waterhole cried—adding quickly, "*Sauvez les Grenouilles!*\*"

---

\* He was aware that the Beavers assumed anything said in Frog merely repeated what had been said in Beaver. It was convenient when you had something tricky to say.

He then instructed his old friend Maurice Strongarm to spend a billion clams on Petro-Swamp, which wouldn't produce any Swampoil but would make the Beavers feel better.

"But Peter, how will we pay for this?" inquired Jim Cute, the *Eminence Grise** of the Gliberal Party.

He was particularly interested because he was running as a Gliberal in Speed-By-Me riding in Beaverville and had gone to a lot of trouble to have the present member rewarded with a seat in the Sendit.† The Gliberals hadn't lost the Speed-By-Me riding in 20 years but Jim Cute wasn't taking any chances.

"Let MacKick'Em worry about that," replied Peter Waterhole. "When we needed clams for the Frogs, we took them from the Beavers. Now that we need them for the Beavers, we'll take them from the Marmots. MacKick'Em will find a way."

*Fr.: Greasy Eminence.

†The Upper House in the Swamp, so named because, when any matter was brought before it, the members would send it to committee. Members were called Senders and were highly respected. They were even more highly paid.

Allan MacKick'Em was the Finance Minister of the Swamp and, though he was dull, he was very shrewd. Everyone was confident that he would indeed find a way to take the Marmots' clams.

"Now, grab that oil," Peter Waterhole told his Energy Minister, Marc La Pond. "We'll have no more Lowspeeds."

He referred, of course, to Peter Lowspeed, leader of the Marmots and the Chief Minister's archenemy.

His Energy Minister, like himself, had been educated by the Jeez-You-Wits and had a mind as sharp as a woodpecker's bill. Peter had no doubt that La Pond would out-think Lowspeed, the former halfback—or *demi-derrière,* as Peter Waterhole called him in Frog.

But he had not reckoned with the treacherous nature of the Marmot leader, who responded by shutting the valve on the great wooden pipeline.

The Chief Minister was apoplectic and dispatched Marc La Pond to straighten out Lowspeed and the Marmots' energy minister, Merv Leak.

Friendly News Animals were spoken to and stories began appearing about the Greedy Marmots and the grand statesmanship of Peter Waterhole. Peter Newspeak at *Mapleleaf* magazine, which had been more or less created by the Gliberal Party, was highly sympathetic. For a while the Gliberals' Wallop Pole rating went up beautifully. It seemed like Old Times.

"Rally round the Dam!" they cried. "Hurray for the Dam!"

But alas, there were now many dams in the Swamp and the other animals no longer responded to the old cry. Worse still, most of the other Tribal Leaders joined Lowspeed in his treachery and soon voices across the Swamp were raised against Peter Waterhole.

"We must prepare for the day when the Swampoil is gone," said the Marmots.

"We have long been poorer than you," said the Codfish. "Now we must build our own future."

"What have you ever done for us?" asked the Otters.

Peter Waterhole was furious.

What could he do with these selfish animals? How could he make them share his dream? .

Then one day, while sitting beside the pool in his home at 24 Nossex Drive, the idea hit him. He would build a Monument!

A Monument to inspire the Swamp and make the animals forget about fighting."

"There'll be a statue of me at the top," he said excitedly. "And at the bottom I will enshrine the Sacred Birchbark with the Constitution written on it."

Then, looking at his reflection in the pool, he began striking poses.

"Perhaps something like General de Gall," he murmured.

Although he had endured some differences with the General, Peter admired his style.

"No, a bit too military," he decided. Having been unavoidably absent from the Great Animal War, Peter Waterhole was always slightly uneasy about military matters.

Or Machovelli, the great thinker whom he admired so much. No, the Ordinary Animals wouldn't understand.

"Perhaps a toga," he said throwing a towel around himself. "Caesar! Law Giver, Empire Builder, Conqueror of Lesser Animals . . . not bad . . . and the nose is right.

"Or Napoleon Blown-Apart!"

He thrust his hand dramatically into his bathing robe.

"It feels right," he said.

But no . . . the military thing. Pity.

Then he had it! Of course—Louis the Sun King, the Most Glorious Monarch in History!

He strode across the lawn to the top of the cliff overlooking the Nottalot River and raised his arm in triumph.

"*Le Swamp, c'est moi!*" he cried.

Full of new energy, Peter Waterhole hurried to his basement and began work on the Monument with furious enthusiasm.

Nothing else mattered. The running of the Swamp was left to La Pond and Jean Crouton and Allan MacKick'Em. Petty day-to-day routine bored Peter Waterhole anyway.

"Who knows what to do about the economy?" he muttered as he seized a chisel.

"Who cares about the Tribal Leaders?" he said as the chips started to fly from an enormous block of maple.

Hour after hour, day after day, he laboured. Gradually the heroic form took shape.

Larger than life.

"After all, that's the way I am," Peter said modestly.

From time to time he gave thought to the words to be written on the Sacred Birchbark, noble words already engraved in his mind. Peter Waterhole, you see, was a Lowyer,[*]

and all his life he had dreamed of giving the Swamp a Constitution. As a Yackademic, he had written books about it, and now he saw his dream coming true.

It would be necessary to have a conference, of course, and listen to a lot of tedious ideas from Ordinary Animals.

And the Tribal Leaders would make trouble as usual, especially Peter Lowspeed.

"Big hat, small mind," Peter Waterhole grumbled as he thought about the Marmot leader.

His critics were clearly irrational. "How can a Constitution be un-Constitutional?" he said indignantly.

No matter, he would have his way in the end because the Gliberal Party was made up mostly of Lowyers and they all believed in words on birchbark.

___

[*] An animal who dealt with rules written on birchbark; so named, some said, because they got to the bottom of things. Some had other explanations.

So the Great Debate began.

Ed Broadlybent and the Trendy P were boisterously happy, because here was a cause both noble and theoretical—just their sort of thing.

Joe Hoo, the befuddled Owl who was Leader of the Hapless Preservatives, couldn't see a clear answer.

"We can do better," he cried on some occasions.

"The whole thing is nonsense," he said on others, and led a Phillip Buster.*

Peter Waterhole came up out of the ground from time to time to take part in the debate, but mostly he worked on the Monument.

As he toiled, a greater dream took shape in his mind.

"This will be the beginning of a New Swamp!" he said. "Greater than anything Sir John A. Macbeaver ever imagined."

He would bring order and logic to the untidy Swamp.

Perhaps he would even drain it.

He would raise up even more intelligent Civil Serpents to lead the New Swamp, even more energetic Bureaucrabs to pass on their orders, and still more loyal Snivel Servants to carry them out.

Other animals in distant lands like Margaret Hatchet and Ronald Ray-Gun might take the axe to their bureaucracies but he would show what real government could accomplish. His would be strong and centralized, similar to that which had given the Homeland of the Frogs its worldwide reputation.

"*My* kind of Swamp!" Peter Waterhole shouted.

*Debating tactic named after the famous holdup man, Phil Buster.

First it was necessary to get the old Constitution back from the Land of the Bulldogs, so off he went to have tea with Mrs. Hatchet.

"Sorry to bother you," he said.

"No trouble at all," she said. "One lump or two?"

No need to bother her with details, he thought, so they chatted about the weather and the children.

"Well, rightie-oh," she said finally. "Must be off. I'll have them look for that thing—what's it called again?"

"The Bulldog Swampian Act," said Peter Waterhole.

"Oh yes, of course," she said. "We don't have a Constitution, you know. I wonder where they put yours. Must be around somewhere. Well, cheerie-bye."

Off she pattered, and Peter Waterhole went back to his important work.

As he laboured, he planned the raising of the Monument. It would be the greatest occasion in the history of the Swamp.

The Leaders of the world must be there!

How could he get them to come?

Yes, of course. A conference. About what? He considered the possibilities.

"I've got it!" he exclaimed. "I'll become the champion of the Poor Animals of the world. Take from the rich and give to the poor—just as I'm doing with the Marmots and the Beavers. I'll be a modern-day Robin Hoodwink.

"Maybe they'll give me the Noble Prize!"

He was delighted with the whole idea. It was the sort of thing he had dreamed of as a student at the Sorebum and at the Bulldog School of Wreckonomics; what they had talked of at the great Come-You-Nits Conference.

What the Swamp needed was a Monument *and* a Great Cause. Peter Waterhole would give it both.

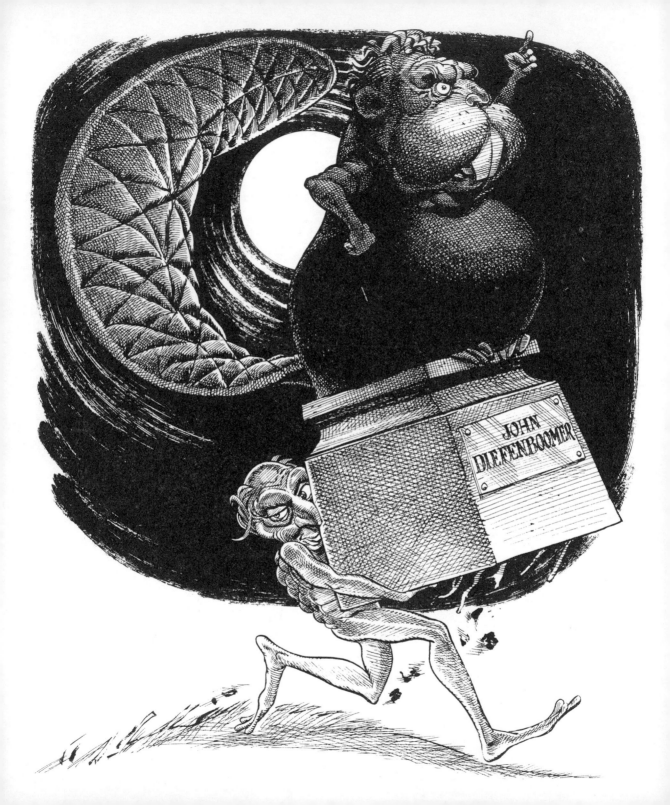

So off he went to meet some Poor Animals; along the way, he thought he might as well get in some sliding in the Yelps Mountains.

While he was in those perilous mountains, disaster struck—and it revealed the true spirit of Peter Waterhole.

He was trapped by giant snow slides!

A lesser animal might have been paralyzed by fear, but not Peter Waterhole. By carrier pigeon, brave messages escaped.

"Wine running low," one said ominously.

"Out of fresh fish," said another.

The Poor Animals of the south, eagerly awaiting their champion, were so dazzled that, when he finally arrived, no one felt worthy to meet him.

Peter Waterhole was deeply moved.

Soon, he returned to Nottalot and his great work. He imagined places where his Monument might be raised. For example, at the top of the hill beside the Fleece Tower along with Sir John A. Macbeaver and Sir Wilfred Laureate. The other statues there would have to be moved, of course, but they weren't very important anyway.

As he worked, the words of Napoleon Blown-Apart came to him once again: "The only battle that counts is the last one."

Everything was becoming clear in his mind. His last important act in the Swamp would be the raising of the Monument and the enshrining of the Sacred Birchbark. It would all happen on the Swamp's National Day. And the Leaders of the world would come. They would be so impressed that they would make him Secretary General of All the Animals.

The entire Swampian army would march past—maybe even twice since there was so little of it left. The Royal Swampian Mounted Police would put on their act. All the bands in the Swamp would play at the same time. And Bobby Jim-Jam would play his famous "Swamp-Pa-Pa" song.

Making the Beavers rich again would have to wait.

But as the days went by, messengers arrived from time to time; the news they brought was bad and grew steadily worse. The bottom was falling out of the Swamp—and the clam was falling out the bottom.

And then, word came of a new problem. The water level behind the Dam was dropping alarmingly, especially at the Beavers' end.

What could be happening?

Gerald Gooey of the All-Swamp Bank said that it was lack of liquidity caused by excessive resource base outflow compounded by insufficient initial through-put.

"Very wise," said the Media Animals.

"Push-pull inflationary stagnation," said the C. D. Howl Institute.

"Very probably," agreed the Editorial Writers.

"Not enough water," said the Ordinary Animals—but no one paid any attention.

Marc La Pond said it was caused by the Marmots turning off the Swampoil pipeline.

"Because of them," he said, "it will be necessary to impose a tax."

So the Marmots became even more unpopular, and the Gliberals prepared for their triumph.

It turned out in the end that the Marmots *were* the problem: they had dug a giant lake to store their clams, and the waters of the Swamp were draining into it.

Faced with such grave problems a lesser animal might have panicked, but Peter Waterhole coolly laboured on. He had the tallest tree in the Land of the Otters cut down for the column of the statue—to the annoyance of the Otters who had been fond of it—and he kept right on chiselling.

Until one day his secretary came into the studio. Peter Waterhole looked up in irritation.

"Sorry to disturb you, sir—the Solicitous General is here. He says it's urgent."

"What's his name?" asked Peter, who was having difficulty remembering the names of his junior ministers.

"He didn't say, sir."

"Well, show him in."

In came Robert Cap-In-Hand, eyes wide with terror, clutching a report.

"The Sublime Court," he gasped. "The Sublime Court, they're going on holiday."

"So?"

"They're not going to decide on the Constitution until they get back."

Peter Waterhole staggered backward, dropping his chisel. Then he hurled his mallet across the room.

"They can't do this to me!" he screamed. "Everything will be ruined!"

Now, the Swampian National Day would pass before he could get the old Constitution back from the Bulldogs.

The World Leaders would come before the Sacred Birchbark was ready.

"What kind of system do we have," he groaned, "when judges can't be trusted?"

So it happened that the great celebrations were cancelled.

But the the World Leaders came anyway.

Frankly, they were not terribly impressed with North-South Chat.

"We've been trying it for 35 years," they said.

"The Swamp will lead by giving away more clams," promised Peter Waterhole.

"But where will you get them?" asked the World Leaders.

"From the Marmots," said Peter Waterhole.

"Well . . ." they replied, and finally put into the official communiqué that, under certain circumstances, they might consider doing something.

"Victory!" cried Peter Waterhole's press officers, and the Media Animals loyally reported it.

But Peter knew things were not going well.

The clam was dropping through the bottom of the Swamp and even the Ordinary Animals were beginning to complain.

"It's all the fault of the Energy Plan," the Tribal Leaders cried, and refused to talk about the Sacred Birchbark any more.

Peter Waterhole was furious and went off in a S.N.I.T.*

Everything was coming apart.

By now he should have triumphed. He had already scheduled a victory holiday, after which he would retire as Father of the New Swamp—and take up his new post with the United Animals.

So, in high ill-humour, he left for the Royal Wedding.

"Just like the Bulldogs to upstage me," he complained.

From the Land of the Bulldogs, in accordance with his long-standing plan, he went to far-off Can-Ya to inspire the Poor Animals by giving away money.

"After all," he said reasonably, "our clams don't cost much."

"Very true," nodded the Media Animals wisely.

* Small vehicle made in the Homeland of the Frogs by the Société Nationale des Industries de Transport.

Back in the sinking Swamp, Joe Hoo demanded that the Chief Minister return to Nottalot to face the clam crisis, but how could he? After all, he had been invited on safari by none other than Adnan Cash-Only, the famous Camel arms dealer and intellectual. How could Joe Hoo understand the importance of such a man as that?

So, along with his sons Just-In, Just-Out and Pasha, he went off into the wilderness.

Adnan Cash-Only proved to be a gracious host and sparkling conversationalist.

"You want to buy some hot scout wagons?" he asked as they sat sipping wine and roughing it. "Very good for putting down insurrections."

Peter Waterhole thanked him but said he already had a lot. Besides, his cash was gone.

"Pity," said Adnan. "Maybe some flame throwers? Very nice. Very cheap."

Peter would have gladly stayed on but, alas, duty called and he returned to the humdrum life of Nottalot.

"Perhaps," he reasoned, "it's better to be a big frog in a small pond . . ."

On his return, there were the usual nitpicking questions; he sighed and shrugged and tried to make the animals see reason.

"Can't you see we have obligations to the Poor Animals?" he asked.

"But we are the Poor," said a voice from the rear.

What could you do with animals like that?

At the Chief Minister's Office, his Cabinet Animals and officials were waiting, wringing their tails in anguish.

What could they do?

Jim Cute's noble crusade in Speed-By-Me had failed.

Marc La Pond had used all his Jeez-You-Wit logic and failed.

Allan MacKick'Em had tried to buy the Swamp and failed.

Jean Crouton's charm had no effect. Mark MacFidget's degrees had not helped.

Even Team Swamp had let him down.

Now, the Gliberals had made so many deals with the Tribal Lands that they couldn't remember them all let alone afford them.

Peter Waterhole was furious. *He* had never had any trouble with money.

"Peter," said Marc La Pond firmly, "there's only one thing left. You must erect the Monument."

"But it's not ready," he cried.

"Raise it anyway," said La Pond.

"Without the Sacred Birchbark?" asked Peter.

"We've got to do something," said La Pond. "Otherwise they'll throw us out."

Sadly, Peter Waterhole agreed.

The next week Snivel Servants and Bureaucrabs loyally trooped into the meadow in front of the Fleece Tower. The entire Swampian army was mustered. And the RSMP were given the day off from investigating disloyal animals. Peter Waterhole stood on the dais with the senior Civil Serpents and the Cabinet Animals, while the band of the Swampian Guards played music from the land of the Eagles and the Bulldogs. The Bureaucrabs below scurried sideways making sure all was in readiness.

"Ready?" cried Jim Cute.

"Any time you say, JC," yelled the Bureaucrabs.

"Pull!" shouted Peter Waterhole.

"But not too hard," cautioned the USLES officials.

"It's leaning to the right," shouted Peter Waterhole. "Pull harder on the left."

"No," said the USLES officials, "Don't pull so hard on the right."

Gradually, shakily, the Great Monument rose into the air as the rain fell and a mass choir sang "O Swamp" in many versions.

Peter Waterhole was delighted, and the following day he went out to get the reaction of the Ordinary Animals.

"How do you like it?" he asked.

"Like what?" the animals replied.

"The Monument," he said, suppressing his irritation.

"It's all right. But what does it do?"

"It doesn't *do* anything," he snapped. "It inspires you!"

The Ordinary Animals shrugged and Peter Waterhole hopped off muttering that General de Gall had been right when he said, "I love my Land but I dislike the Animals."

In the days that followed, as the Ordinary Animals went about their business, they occasionally glanced up at the Monument.

Soon they noticed something different about it.

"Is it as high as it used to be?" they asked each other.

The Monument was sinking!

Some of the animals laughed. But the Snivel Servants rushed to tell the Bureaucrabs who scurried to tell the Civil Serpents who slithered to Michael Pitstop who raced to Peter Waterhole who was in the pool at 24 Nossex.

"It's sinking!" Michael Pitstop cried.

"Nonsense! The clam can't sink any further," said Peter Waterhole.

"No! The MONUMENT!!" gasped Pitstop.

"Declare a National Emergency!" choked Peter Waterhole. "Who's the Minister of Swampian Defense? Call out the army!"

He and Pitstop raced to the scene of the disaster, where Swampian Works employees were watching with fascination as the shaft slowly sank into the mud.

"DO SOMETHING!!!" screeched Peter Waterhole.

"Do anything!" screamed Bureaucrabs running to the scene.

"Charge!" bellowed the generals, and the army charged.

But try as they might to stop it, the Monument continued to sink.

Faster.

And faster.

AND FASTER.

Until all that remained was the extended finger of Peter Waterhole.

Then, it was gone.

Almost immediately, a strange, peaceful feeling settled over the Swamp.

Animals looked at one another in wonderment. Then, they began to smile. Some began to laugh.

"No more Monuments!" they shouted.

All across the Swamp, the shout was repeated. Animals began to nod their heads wisely and agreed that never again would they allow a Monument builder to run things. "We used to have common sense," some said. "We'll have it again."

And all went better and better in the Swamp until one day, as the sun was setting, some Beavers saw a strange silhouette against the sky above the Great Western Hills.

"What can it be?" they asked.

A Marmot Swampoil machine?

No, it seemed bigger.

The Beavers gathered in little groups to discuss this strange new sight.

Then one animal came by with a wooden telescope.

Suddenly, everyone knew what it was.

W9-CGY-761

WATCHUNG

# Henry and Mudge
## AND THE
# Forever Sea

*The Sixth Book of Their Adventures*

*Story by Cynthia Rylant*
*Pictures by Suçie Stevenson*

SIMON & SCHUSTER BOOKS FOR YOUNG READERS

Somerset County Library
Bridgewater, NJ  08807

To Cheryl and Marc—CR
For Walker—SS


**THE HENRY AND MUDGE BOOKS**

SIMON & SCHUSTER BOOKS FOR YOUNG READERS
An imprint of Simon & Schuster Children's Publishing Division
1230 Avenue of the Americas
New York, New York 10020
Text copyright © 1989 by Cynthia Rylant
llustrations copyright © 1989 by Suçie Stevenson
SIMON & SCHUSTER BOOKS FOR YOUNG READERS is a trademark of Simon & Schuster.

All rights reserved including the right of reproduction in whole or in part of any form.
READY-TO-READ is a registered trademark of Simon & Schuster, Inc.

The text of this book is set in 18-point Goudy
The illustrations are rendered in pen-and-ink and watercolor
Printed and bound in the United States of America

10  9  8  7  6  5  4  3

The Library of Congress has cataloged the hardcover edition as follows:
Rylant, Cynthia.
Henry and Mudge and the forever sea: the sixth book of their
adventures / story by Cynthia Rylant : pictures by Suçie Stevenson.
p.   cm.
Summary: Follows the seaside adventures of Henry, Henry's father,
and Henry's big dog Mudge.
[1. Seashore –Fiction.  2. Dogs—Fiction.  3. Fathers and sons—
Fiction.] I. Stevenson, Suçie, ill.  II. Title
[PZ7.R982Hf    1993]
[E]-dc20                          92-28646
ISBN 0-689-81016-4 (hc)    0-689-81017-2 (pbk)

# Contents

# To the Beach

It was summer vacation
and Henry and his big dog Mudge
were going to the beach.
Mudge had never been
to the beach.

Henry promised

he would like it.

"You'll like the waves,"

he said.

"And the sand castles.

And the shells.

But don't drink the water!"

he warned.

"Too salty!"

They went in the car
with Henry's father.
In Henry's bag were
green goggles,
a yellow bucket,
an orange shovel,
and a dump truck.

In Mudge's bag were
a blue bowl,
a jug of water,
half of a bone,
and a tennis ball.

In Henry's father's bag were
a book about shells,
six towels,
and a red rubber lobster
he liked
to bring along.

They sang sea songs
all the way.
Henry's father said
"Yo-ho-ho"
about a hundred times.
Henry acted like a shark.
Mudge just wagged.
They couldn't wait
to get there.

# The Forever Sea

"I see it!" Henry shouted.
The ocean was waiting.
It was blue
and white
and forever.

Henry's father
honked the car horn.
Mudge barked.
They parked the car
and ran for the sand.

Mudge got there first.
He ran right into
the water.
SPLASH!

Henry was second.

SPLASH!

Henry's father was third.

SPLASH!

The white foam
rushed
around their legs.
They laughed and hopped
and ran.

18

A big wave
knocked Henry down.
He rolled
all the way
back to shore.

"Wow," said Henry.
He got up
and ran back in.

Henry's father
rode a wave
like he was
a surfboard.

He rode it
all the way
back to shore.
"Wow," he said.
He got up
and ran back in.

Mudge was not as brave
as Henry and Henry's father.
He just ran
along the edge.
He stayed out
of the big waves.

But still he got
so wet
that he looked like
a whale with legs.

They all played
a long time.

# Brave Dog

For lunch,
Henry and Mudge
and Henry's father
walked to a hot dog stand.

Henry had a hot dog
with ketchup.
Henry's father had a hot dog
with ketchup
and mustard
and onions
and slaw
and chili
and cheese.

"Yuck," said Henry.

Mudge had three hot dogs.

Plain.

In one gulp.

After lunch,
Henry and his father
began to build
a sand castle.

Henry made the moats.

Henry's father made the towers.

Mudge made a nice bed
and went to sleep.

When the castle was finished,
Henry's father
stuck his red rubber lobster
on the tallest tower.
Then he and Henry
clapped their hands.

Suddenly

a giant wave

washed far on the sand

and it covered everything.

It covered the moats.

It covered the towers.

It covered Mudge, who woke up.

"Oops," said Henry.

"Save that lobster!"
cried Henry's father.
The water was pulling it
out to sea.

Mudge ran and jumped
into the waves.
He caught the lobster
before it was lost forever.

"Good dog!" said Henry's father.

"Brave dog!" said Henry.

They all had cherry sno-cones

to celebrate.

# Good-bye, Crab

At the end of the day
it was time
to say good-bye
to the ocean.

Henry and Mudge
and Henry's father
walked along the sand,
watching the
orange sun set,
watching the
water sparkle
green and yellow.

Suddenly,

a crab popped out

from under the sand.

It came up sideways,

very fast.

So fast that Mudge

nearly stepped on it.

"Look out, Mudge!"
Henry said.
Mudge stopped
and put his nose
to the sand.
The crab looked at him.
He looked at the crab.

42

"I can't tell if that is
the front of the crab
or the back of the crab,"
said Henry's father.

Suddenly the crab ran,
sideways,
away from them.

Mudge chased it.
It popped back
under the sand.

44

Henry looked at its
new hole.
"Wow," he said.
"Wow," said his father.

Mudge stuck his nose
into the hole.
But nobody came out.

"Since we can't have
crab for dinner,"
said Henry's father,
"I guess we'll have
to have
another cherry sno-cone."

Henry cheered and hugged him.
As they walked down the sand,
Mudge stuck his nose
into every hole he saw.

But nobody

ever came out.

E READER RYLANT
Rylant, Cynthia.
Henry and Mudge and the
forever sea : the sixth
WGL      696312

WATCHUNG PUBLIC LIBRARY
12 STIRLING ROAD
WATCHUNG, NEW JERSEY 07060